Confessions of a Special Needs Dad:

Honesty and Hope for the Journey

By Andrew's Dad

www.specialneedsdadchronicles.com

Confessions of a Special Needs Dad:
Honesty and Hope for the Journey
By Andrew's Dad

ISBN-13: 978-1987676136
ISBN-10: 1987676130

Published by Speckled Leaf Press.

Printed in the United States of America

www.specialneedsdadchronicles.com

This book is dedicated to Adam M.
for his encouragement, prayers and
friendship on this project and to all the
Special Needs Dads along the journey.
Hold fast. Hang tight.

Introduction

I began writing a blog called www.specialneedsdad-chronicles.com a few years ago after I noticed a gaping hole in resources for special needs dads. And by resources, I don't just mean medical books or sites to help in a Psychology 101 way, but also books or blogs where special needs dads could hear the stories of others, could share in their pain and their healing. A place vacant of petty meme wisdom or vapid sayings. A place where honesty and hope were part of the narrative.

This book is a compendium of those blogs. I have only lightly edited for clarity and continuity and, out of respect, for how I felt at the time, I have not changed anything to reflect how I feel now, only because I feel it is critical to keep that authenticity to the text. I also have not polished and re-written each blog for the same reason.

A few notes before we get started. My son Andrew has a host of medical conditions. The most prevalent one is Cri du chat syndrome which means he is missing part of his fifth chromosome. His condition is on the cellular level and the absence of that part of the chromosome causes mild to severe mental and physical disabilities.

We did not know he had this condition until after he was born. When he was born, we were told he would never walk or talk.

A few notes on abbreviations and acronyms.

1. I refer to our special needs child as Andrew. His brother is referred to as Peter. Since I write my blog quasi-anonymously, we have preferred to keep that model here. The same for my name as author and my wife's name.

2. When I occasionally use the term SN it refers to special needs. SND as is special needs dad, SN children for special needs children, et al.

3. This book is not sequential or chronological. I placed them in an order I thought will work. You will also notice that most of the chapters begin when he was around 8-years-old, which was the first time I could finally address these issues.

This book is divided into two sections. The first is on honesty and hope and spans the last ten years that I have been a father of a special needs child. The second part is a section called, 'That's what She Said,' which is a compilation of guest blogs written by my wife.

I believe this book is a good companion not only for the special needs dad, but also for their extended family members and friends. I think many times, as special needs parents, we are afraid or reticent or too defensive to share our thoughts on our life. Maybe this book can help give them a window into our world. Wherever you are calling from, I hope this book gives you a boost along your journey.

Take care. Hold Fast. Be strong.

PART ONE

Honesty & HOPE

Keeping it real along the journey

This is not a story of success, but of waves of successes — some tiny and some gigantic — and more importantly this is a story that is a testament to endurance and the power of prayer and having faith when there is no reason to and pushing into the darkness without a lamp.

This is not a story of illumination, but does have illuminations and ultimately has a resolution or at least a stab at a resolution. This is not a story of finding truth but of finding truths and glimpses of truth and having faith and having doubt.

This is my story, but this is your story, too, if you are a special needs dad, or know someone who is the father of a special needs child or, in many cases, if you have struggled with anything heartbreaking or heart-wrenching or felt cold, clinging darkness hanging on your shoulders, even on the sunniest of days.

Some may call this blasphemous or too real or too raw. But, before you cast any stones, read the bluntness of Job, the raw evocative accusing of David, the candidness of Christ.

With that read, you've probably deduced that this book does contain elements of Christianity. I do not pronounce myself an amazing pious Christian who has a monopoly on Truth and is filled with answers and radiate glory and optimism.

I am a believer, though, most of the time. My faith I hesitate to admit owes as much as to Pascal's Wager as to mysticism and miracles. I do the best I can, some of the time. I believe that grace, mercy, love and hope are what the Good News is all about, and I lean on those more than any doctrine, dogma or other creed.

In other words, when I talk about the Bible and Christ, I say it as someone who is broken, but believes there can be mending. I do not claim to know everything, but, at the same time, I am not naïve or ignorant of science or Atheism (am a former atheist myself) or the myriad of humanistic philosophies or moral relativism.

BRAVING
THE NEW WORLD

Everything has changed. Don't despair. You will make it. Everything is not lost, but everything has changed. How you eat. When you sleep. If you sleep. How you vacation. Your job. Your priorities. Everything.

An example is the familiar cookout. Old friends coming together over drinks. The jokes used and reused are still funny, but comfortable and comforting, like a pair of old slippers. The thick plumes of charcoal smoke shooting from grills. Children laughing and splashing in the pool. You can find yourself sinking back into your old life.

And you might try it once, but, ultimately you can't go again without taking your new self with you.

You can't go because you can't enjoy yourself. You find it harder to relate. The base of sharing is nil.

When your 8-year-old is not toilet trained. When you have to keep him strapped in a wheelchair so he won't strike out or flail at another kid. When you have to constantly monitor him so he won't hit his brother for the

1,000th time and you have to counsel that brother when he says he hates his brother because he has special needs, well, that makes it hard to hold your Solo cup and nibble at your burger and engage in talk on football or work or join in the latest discussion on technology or pop culture.

Your world is not completely centered around your special needs child, but it is affected. Easy jocularity, complaints of having to change a 1-year-old's diapers and hearing about how someone loves Ricky Gervais (despite his disdain and condescension of the special needs population), make it hard to engage or relax. You feel the ebb and flow of the conversation float over you and see yourself stuck on a spit of sand watching it all. You can still fake a laugh, extend a hand and grab a cold one, but it is all a joke. And not a funny one. Because the joke is the event when everything with your child seems so terrible and out of place, and the joke is how you feel inside which has the capacity to make you feel like a joke.

Only at the end of the night, when you are home on the couch and your family is in bed and the house is quiet, can you relax. With the sound of stale laughter still in your ears, you swear to never do that again as you reach for solace in the bottom of a bottle.

FIND
YOUR OUTLET

I cannot stress enough how important it is to find a healthy outlet. An outlet for your anger, frustration. An outlet for a way to not only channel these swells of emotions, but also to find an outlet for escape. Pure escapism in itself is tempting. A quick drink, a TV binge, the desire to plunge into any easy sedative to ease the stress and pain is always there. But I recommend something stronger. More constructive.

Like what? Exercise, for example, is a great fighter against depression. You've got these emotions and the best thing one can do is channel them. I find that exercise not only provides a good way to release any pent-up emotions, but, of course, it is healthy as well.

Art is another option. Yeah, I know not everyone is an artist per se. (I love playing guitar and it saves my life some days). But even flinging paint against a canvas and then setting it on fire is better than simmering in unresolved emotion. Art is wide open to interpretation. And that leads me to landscaping. Hate gardening? Okay. Well, then find some trees that need cutting down. And use an old axe. And don't be afraid to unleash a yelp when you fell the tree. Trust me, you will feel better for it and the neighbors can get over it.

There are tons of other outlets that I won't cover, but my point is find something constructive for a distraction, a release, an escape. Hiking. Golf. Woodworking. Otherwise, the temptation is to sit in your despairing state or, worse, turn to quicker and easier means of pleasure to ease the pain on this journey.

Wonder at work in the eyes of a Special Needs Child

This book addresses a lot of the unsaid pain and darkness of being a special needs dad. But it is not all bleak. I believe there is some grace and peace and wonder and miracles not only at the end of everything, but also during the journey.

One theme that resonates with me on what a lot of us are missing in our lives is 'wonder.' It is a theme I will address at length at some point, but in relation to the world of special needs children, I think of Matthew 18:3, where Jesus said we need to be like little children to get into heaven. There is a ton in that one sentence, but the thing that gets me is 'wonder.' Little children have lots of traits that we need to emulate and we have forgotten - openness, joy and, especially, wonder. We need to have wonder in our lives everyday. Cynicism and despair aren't welcome. Worry is not welcome. Wide-eyed curiosity is.

One of the things that Andrew has taught me is grasping and re-grasping that sense of wonder. I see wonder in the eyes of Andrew and other special needs children more than anywhere else. Pure unfiltered joy. Excitement. Not eyeing the horizon, not criticizing the past, but discovering and re-discovering a sense of wonder in every moment. It will not solve all your problems, but learning that lesson from them is a blessing for this journey.

God won't give you more than you can handle & other myths people invented

Do you remember that verse in the Bible about, "God won't give you more than you can handle"?

No, neither do I. You know why? It doesn't exist. Yep. Just another quaint phrase invented by a Pollyanna well-wisher, a preacher to appease his congregation, a zealot to assuage rage or, perhaps even if I am more gentle in my judgment, just someone trying to help someone get through a hard time.

But, it is not Biblical. Kind of the like the old phrase, "every tub sits on its own bottom." Sorry, folks. That is an English proverb. Not from the Bible either.

But, candidly, even if you take Biblical effort out of the phrase, "God won't give you more than you can handle," it is offensive, insensitive and callous.

Can you tell this phrase strikes a nerve?

Why is that?

When Andrew was born and my world was turned inside out, the very foundations of reality shifted, my script rewrote, hearing a pithy phrase like this was enough to raise my blood pressure.

I wanted to yell, "That is complete bull! This is made-up Hallmark crap! I am hanging on by a thread. By an eyelash. And you, in your meme wisdom, dare to tell me some empty notion like this! As if this knee-jerk phrase should be enough to make all right with the world."

I never did do that. Not to anyone's face, though I did nurse the grudge many times alone and have poured it out through the windows of my car while driving to work at times.

It is so patronizing. Like, "God gives special needs kids to special parents."

Where did they come from? No one gets made for this. No one who comes into this sphere of being has a built-in switch they've been waiting to use called the "Special Needs Parent" switch. No, when we find out our child has special needs, that our child will never have a shot at 'normal' or living a typical life, we are shot up, beat and bent, and our emotions are twisted and our faith wrenched. We find no comfort or hope in a phrase like that. We don't want to be special and, God knows, we never wanted our children to have special needs.

It goes hand-in-hand with the old saying, "I don't see how you do it." A phrase that is never a question, but a statement, perhaps of admiration, but it can drive one crazy. I mean, I have restrained myself for the most part and left with a, "We're all doing the best we can," but what I've wanted to reply is:

You don't see how I do it? I don't know how I do it.

You don't see how I do it? Well, what are my options?

Escape to Narnia? Push the pause button on life?

Move to Mars?

Suicide?

You don't see how I do it? Again, the divorce rates for special needs parents hovers around 80 percent and the suicide rate for special needs dads is extremely higher than average. Don't tell me you don't see how I do it. I really, some days, don't know how I do it either.

My apologies for the aforementioned sarcasm, but that is the way it is.

So, there it is. My rant on this is over. Where does that leave us? What should you say to a parent of a special needs child? Sometimes everything. Sometimes nothing. We – and I say this collectively – don't want to be pitied. We don't want to be praised. We want – much like our children – to simply be accepted.

TODAY is the best day ever

Andrew has many key phrases he uses almost like mantras.

He calls many of his outings with me – kicking the soccer ball, playing the guitar or bongos or going to the park – an "adventure" as in, "I want a soccer adventure" or "Let's have a musical adventure."

It adds a pleasant touch to the old, "Let's go to the park." Instead, it is, as I imagine it should be rightly called, an "adventure."

After all, it was Tolkien who said it is a dangerous thing going out of one's front door.

But, Andrew has another phrase he uses often.

And it is hands down my favorite. Whenever we have an 'adventure' or daddy time or visits with family and friends and I ask him how he is doing or how his day was, he often says, "Today is the best day ever."

I love that expression. Why? Because in the grand scheme of things, today is the best day ever, because today is the only day ever. To paraphrase a cliché, the past is history and the future does not exist. This moment – this here and now is all there is – and all that ultimately matters.

Andrew's outlook captures that sentiment. One of the gifts that special needs children give us is the ability to see many things as they truly are – unfiltered by anxiety or regret, unspoiled by regrets and absorbing pure joy – despite how big or small that joy is – wherever it is found.

That is a lesson I need to be re-taught daily, or almost hourly. That perspective is really the only perspective. Like many things in life, though, it is not for only us to realize, but try to pass it on to others.

15 minutes at a time

Most people don't know what to say when they discover you have a special needs child, and the fact is I don't talk to most people about it (as odd as it is as this is open for anyone to read, I still don't talk to most people about it).

But, in the wake of Andrew's birth, I really, adamantly didn't talk to anyone outside of my wife those first few months. Too much confusion in me. Too much rage. Too much of a chance for the short fuse in me to be lit. And I didn't want that, and I knew that they wouldn't want it either.

I caught a few of the clichéd sayings but tried to ignore them. Would do almost anything I could not to strike out. Buried my feelings in myself.

Then there was my Uncle Mike. He invited me to dinner. I gave Uncle Mike the exception. Within a five year period, Uncle Mike had lost one son to drowning in a bizarre boating accident and another to suicide. He was single, divorced and alone in this world. He had seen the dark side of life – seen? He had experienced it - and was still living through it. He had the fortitude to push forward with amazing resilience.

We sat at a corner booth in an Applebee's, of all places to discuss the struggles and emptiness of life. Mike gave me a few pieces of advice then. One, he said, was when people give you the empty platitudes, just to smile and nod and walk away. Secondly, he said, some people say, "One day at a time." That's good, but he said on a bad day, he would go:

"15 minutes at a time."

It is a mantra and practice I have adopted on dark days. Just try to get through the next 15 minutes, then the next 15 minutes. Maybe eventually the next hour. You think about the future and you can be beyond overwhelmed. You think about the present and you can feel the same way. Just 15 minutes at a time. You will make it. Then, maybe, when you're ready, one day at a time. But start small.

Into The Cave is okay

There is a time for everything under the sun, the Prophet wrote in Ecclesiastes and that saying has been phrased and re-phrased through the years by writers and philosophers much more profound than I.

With that said, in the wake of finding out your child has special needs, there is a time to lay on the mat. To mend. To find out what just happened. To shake off the shock. To stay out of the light. To protect yourself and your fragile emotions, your shattered state of mind. To stay in The Cave as I call it.

Time spent in The Cave can be good. It is often necessary. You can take that time to weave new emotional and spiritual sinews over broken bones, or rather, broken dreams. Time to learn how to cope with your new reality. Time to gain fortitude for when you emerge.

That is fine.

Do not force yourself to rush back into the world armed with false bravado, empty quotes or a hollow chest. After Andrew was born, I withdrew to a tremendous degree – more so now than I realized it then. Was it healthy? I don't know.

I just know I had to do it. I would ignore a phone call from a friend, yet would respond with an email that usually said something like, "I love you and I appreciate you, but I can't talk right now." And that is the truth. I couldn't. I couldn't engage in small talk. I could barely summon a facade to go to work some days. I was broken. I wanted these people reaching out to me to know that I desperately loved them and appreciated them. But, I wasn't ready. In person, at family events or an unforeseen run-in with an old friend, any words that fell out of my mouth were noncommittal, shallow and if someone asked me how I was doing, I became beyond adept at changing the subject quickly.

(A word here before I go on: 'In The Cave' does not mean shutting down communication with your wife or dissociating from your child or children, but, rather, taking the time, the steps, the necessary thoughts for you to face the world not only as a man, but as a husband and father.)

So I hid in my Cave. I didn't trust myself with my emotions. Too much rage. Too much confusion. Too raw. I did not get on Facebook for years for that very reason. I avoided social settings at all costs. I would have never dreamed of starting a blog about the experience - it would have been nothing but profanities, rage and vitriolic-laced tirades against everything. I didn't take phone calls. I rarely made any. I could not explain – well, anything - to anyone - even myself. I did not want to talk about my life. I did not want to venture down the path of – real or perceived - self-pity with them. I had no blanking idea what to say. I rarely visited with old friends – and only then a couple whom I knew I could trust to The End. And, even then, there was the understanding – blatantly stated at the outset – that if I wanted to talk about Andrew, I would. Otherwise, that subject was off-limits and the goal was simply to fellowship, to make music, enjoy good food and drink and to get out of the world for a while.

So, I took my time in The Cave.

And then, in due time, I was ready. Not eager, but ready. Ready for reemergence into the greater world with the wound scarred, my mind focused and my new self.

These days, I spend most of my time outside of The Cave. I have learned – not mastered, but learned – how to cope with being a special needs dad and how to relate, or not to relate, to others. To the world. The Cave is always there, though, and sometimes I duck back in to its protective womb when I need to. It is not a Cave of sadness, but has become a place to recharge, to re-energize, to recalibrate.

I am glad I found The Cave when I did. I have seen too many other special needs parents bury their sorrow, ignore it, mask it in sayings they didn't believe or drown it in alcohol or the haze of drugs.

I leave you with this. When you go into your Cave – whether you call it reflection, a place of protection, solitude, etc. – do not make it a permanent residence. At some point, you need to face the world full of its faults, despite the raw nerves of being a special needs dad that may still throb beneath the surface. But, more importantly, you need to face the world to remember there is still breathless beauty, sublime moments, amazing people and unforeseen joy that is well worth leaving the familiarity of solitude for.

Our work outlives us

The great writer and preacher Henri Nouwen once said, "The fruits of your labors may be reaped two generations from now. Trust, even when you don't see the results." That is a phrase worth reading and re-reading, especially when we are in times of strife or doubt or depression raising special needs children. We do not know where the fruits of our efforts will end, what they will accomplish, not only in our lives, not only in our children's lives, but in lives yet to be led, born, envisioned. It is a good thought, a strong thought to harbor and meditate on when you are having a day filled with the calls of doubt or wrestling with the black clouds of despair.

It is a revitalizing thought that whether you are fighting for something as mundane as the bureaucracy of Medicaid or spiritually challenging as encouraging your typical child to keep his chin up, your labor, your work will go on and on and on.

Sometimes just listen

Andrew and I in the dark of the car. A thousand lights on the interstate ahead of us and a smattering of rain and he pulls my hand close to him in the front seat and I realize it is the first time him and I have ever rode in the car at night together. Just the two of us. Side by side in the front seat. He is almost 10. And he tells me that he is a gift from God and usually when he says phrases like this, I ask 'why?' or 'who told you?', because I want to know where he hears these things, how he knows them. I want answers from some Oracle, because I have none. But, this time, I do not ask a question, because I am learning to listen more lately and just to take a blessing as it is. In this dusted and battered world, you have to take what you can when you can and accept it for what it is and that act in itself is in some unholy, yet holy way, a beautiful gift from God.

The alluring call of despair

Andrew had the most violent couple of days he'd had toward me in a couple of years this past Easter weekend.

I still don't know exactly what prompted it, though I think one bout was spurned by anxiety and another caused by a combination of sensory overload and tiredness. But, like many things in the realm of having a special needs child, I have no idea as to the real cause because he simply cannot communicate why.

The violence is one of those aspects of being a special needs dad which possesses many levels of particular pain.

There is the physical pain, the initial literal wounds - getting scratched, bitten, head-butted, punched, hair pulled, etc. As your child grows older - Andrew is now almost 9 - those actions become, of course, more intense in their delivery. And the internal anger and - candidly -

resentment you feel, becomes more intense as well.

The second level, however, is terrible and borderline hideous if you venture to think about it.

It is the fact that a child you love, a child you have sacrificed the last eight years or your life for, a child you have prayed for more than you have prayed for anything else, is assaulting you. I am sure you can sit back and analyze the situation, but that doesn't do a damn bit of good when you're in the middle of a one-way fight.

The situation makes one question the very foundation of everything - that phrase sounds so hyperbolic, but it is true. Any faith, theology, belief in love, logic, belief in making things better, belief in overcoming anything gets turned upside. Later when you are out the situation, you can reflect and analyze and speculate that he was upset, or couldn't communicate or overwhelmed and that is what served as the catalyst for violence. But, many times, even after all that, there is no discernible reason in the aftermath, and even if you can discover a prime mover, a particular cause, it doesn't lessen the emotional and, thus spiritual, wrenching impact of the situation.

I do not have any answer for what to do when this happens or afterwards as a salve or a resolution.

I have gritted my teeth until they have chipped from the sheer force of restraining myself from not striking back.

I have yelled angry prayers at the empty sky.

I have given in and quietly cursed myself and my life.

You can find an outlet and that will help, but, over time, your will to persevere, to be strong, to possess hope can be ground down and the temptation to give in, to give up, grows stronger.

And here is the rub.

It is an easy temptation.

It is not a powerful lure like lust or money or avarice. The temptation to give in is a gentle slope into grey lowlands, a place of mottled grass, of discarded prayers, of forgotten aspirations. Here, apathy and depression walk side by side. If hope is mentioned at all, it is nothing but a stale joke, a thing of another world.

This is the place of despair. I have wandered in its valleys and sat silent in its forgotten lanes cocooned in my numbness.

The challenge is not to dwell there.

The challenge is to not always heed its call.

The challenge is the older you get, the more alluring the call becomes.

Lessons from Lazarus

PART I

One of the strangest passages in the New Testament is about Lazarus, one of Jesus's good friends (John 11: 1-44). Christ waits until after Lazarus dies to visit his family and, then, bring him back to life. I see the miracle aspect as I see many of Christ's miracles – he was empathetic and if He had the ability to heal, by God, he was going to do so.

He healed the blind man. The sick child. But, the key point of this story I want to focus on is the authenticity of the situation. When Jesus arrives at Lazarus's home, he was greeted by many, but, according to most interpretations, he had to summon Mary. One can imagine Mary feeling angry or forlorn. After all, where was this miracle worker, this savior, this one she had honored when her brother was sick? Why didn't He come when they sent messengers for him?

And what did Mary say when she saw him?

Did she praise him with hollow phrases or memorized salutations?

Did she say, "Great one, I have faith in you! From my brother's death, your will is done!"

Did she say, "Our God is an awesome God! You are the best!"

No, she said, and one can imagine quite flatly or accusingly: "Lord, if you had been here, my brother would not have died."

Wow. Period.

How did Jesus react? Did he strike her down? Did he admonish her? Did he tell her to be quiet or not to question him, his motives, his timing?

No, he cried.

There is something in that when it comes to truth-telling. Christ can handle our honesty. Our sadness. Even our accusations. That is stated throughout the Bible in different ways, but I find here it resounds with me on a matter-of-fact level. This is not David weaving poetry in anguish or Job questioning the very nature of the cosmos. This is a simple, almost stoic, accusation as Mary, in essence, says, "Where were you?"

And then the reaction. What did Jesus do? He cried. He did not preach a sermon at that moment. He did not tell her to rejoice. He cried. The truth is He cries with us. He is empathetic. He loves us. Even though there are mysteries that the finite mind cannot grasp, even though His Ways are not always Our Ways, He cares. And He is willing to listen. He does not strike us down for our honesty. We can tell the truth.

Lessons from Lazarus

PART II

I think one of the key lessons from the story of Lazarus (John 11:1-44) is that it is okay to tell the truth to God when we are angry, or bitter or confused. I believe that truth-telling is a pivotal part of survival in one's faith or in one's understanding or misunderstandings of the lessons of Christ and our communication with God.

But there is another lesson from this passage. And it is an age-old lesson from the Good Book. And it is a lesson that is painful.

As it is written, Christ waits until after Lazarus is dead to visit him and his family and bring him back to life.

Reading the passage, it can almost seem like Christ was cold, distant, uncaring, even almost sadistic. Messengers were sent to him: "Jesus, your good friend is dying. Please come save him."

But, He told them, He had work to do and He would be there in time.

In His Time.

And that is the rub of it.

His time is not our time.

The will of the infinite cannot be grasped by the finite mind.

That is all well and good you might say from a philosophical standpoint, but it isn't doing me much good as I wait for my child's behavior to improve, as I wait for Andrew's Medicaid to get approved, as I wait for my friend's child's seizures to cease, as I wait for a door to open so I can allay any worries about how I will pay for Andrew's living when I am gone and buried, as I wait, some days, for Hope itself.

Yet, it is there throughout the Scripture.

His time is not our time.

Frustrating? Yes. But true.

It is Faith in essence.

And with that leap of faith, there is another message here: Hold on. Hang tight. Be strong. Believe.

What God isn't

THE EXPERIENTIAL LESSON

It is much easier sometimes to define what something isn't, than what it is. And playing theology can be a dangerous game if one isn't careful. The older I get and the more I experience, the more I tend to agree with the great preacher and writer Frederick Buechner who said something to the effect that he hopes that God is more amused at our attempts at theology than irritated.

With that said, I have discovered what God isn't. He isn't Harry Potter. You can't summon Him. He doesn't answer prayer, even relentless prayer, with a wave of a wand and fix everything. As C.S. Lewis stated, we pray not to change God, but to change us. That is true and illuminating, but is also harsh.

There is nothing wrong with praying that your child will learn to talk. To walk. To take care of himself. But I have learned as much as I pray for them to be changed and my situation to be changed, I have to pray for myself to change. To change my perspective, to change my patience and my behavior.

That is the one thing I can try to try to control. It is pivotal to my very existence. It is a shame that after 40 years on the planet and reading tons of books on spirituality and religion and tossing about the big names like Paul Tillich, I am only now learning this and yet somehow it had been in front of me the entire time, yet I had overlooked it. Experience trumps philosophy and practice beats pontification.

It's all about the SMALL VICTORIES

I have become a man whose life is defined by small victories, which is not a bad thing, perhaps that is how I should've been looking at life all the way along.

So we take the small victories. A day without your special needs child hitting his brother? Victory! A night without anxiety crippling dreams? Victory! A day when your 9-year-old special needs child actually uses the toilet? Victory!

I experienced a small victory last week. I've been bathing Andrew for over nine years. It is something I am used to by now, it's not even an issue it has become such a part of our routine: The scrubbing, kneeling, bending to wash him. He needs a shower, usually Daddy gets a shower. He needs three showers on a bad day. Hey, Daddy gets three showers. No major issue. You get used to it. That is your reality.

But last week, as I scrubbed his arms for the 1,000th time, as I sang an off-key tune to keep him distracted from the

fear of shampoo getting in his eyes, he said something:
"Thank you for bathing me, Daddy."

Wow. I never expected it. To be thanked. But I took it. And it lit me up and made me smile. And I said, "You're welcome, my son," and planted a kiss upon his undersized head and let the water mingle with my tears.

Small victories.

Bitterness is the greatest enemy

The longer I am a special needs dad, I find that bitterness is one of the fiercest enemies. Anger can be fleeting or can nestle and fester, but will eventually explode internally or externally. Depression can and will linger, but can be fought with medicine, therapy and exercise. Though it might not ever leave, it can be alleviated.

But, bitterness is more of a state of mind. A perspective. And it is a deadly one that combines both anger and depression, along with a dismissal of others and their real or imagined trials.

Example:

I had a colleague the other day tell me how hard it was adjusting back to being in the country after a vacation abroad for a week and that's why they were late on a work related project. I nodded and — bloodless sans emotion or response — proceeded to address the project and get the job done. This is a tactic I use at work to compartmentalize. To get the work done. To not dwell in the mire of the moment.

However, later, and I hate to admit this, I found myself in complete disdain of that person and their excuse. They have a perfect suburban family with two healthy children. The one household income of a spouse is enough to afford gleaming new cars, a home in an upscale neighborhood, and, yes, trips to Europe for couple of weeks.

And they tell me how hard it is being tired.

They live in another universe. They are ignorant of what special needs families go through. On one hand, I should have mercy. Yet, on the other hand, I want to verbally berate them.

"You're tired? You don't know what tired is. My wife has been changing diapers for 11 years. We haven't slept through the night in 11 years because our special needs child gets up every night at least once."

or

"You're tired? You don't know what tired is. My wife totes my special needs child to two to three therapies a week along with his typical sibling. She also works a part-time job. Oh, and by the way, toting him to a therapy generally involves her getting hit, scratched or bitten by special needs child."

and

"You're tired. You don't know what tired is. I still bathe

our special needs child who is ten. I am trying to teach him things like raking or setting the table so one day he might be able to do something, anything with his life. I get attacked every day by my special needs child. I spend over 15 hours a week in the car commuting so my special needs child can go to a special school and work extra side jobs to help pay our ridiculous healthcare. Oh yeah, on top of all of that, I am trying to be a decent husband and raise his brother, a typical child."

In other words, don't tell me how tired you are from returning from a trip from Europe, when I am brain, soul- and bone-weary from a life you know nothing of and would happily take a few punches to the head to get any vacation and would gladly suffer from jet lag.

And yet, and, yet, here is the rub: While what I write is true, those words and thoughts can grow into bitterness, and I know I must not give into bitterness.

It is a strange place to be, in between worlds. I have no desire to open up my heart to people who don't care or wouldn't understand. Yet, perhaps people do need to be educated. All these - and the 1,000 other questions that come with it - are better to be discussed at another time in another book.

In the meantime, I just pray for me to have mercy and to banish that bitter root. Because at the end of the day, it does not taste good nor improve my life or others. Bitterness is a soul killer and can provoke joylessness. It is exclusionary. I fight it and some days am more successful than others. Maybe there is a cure-all. When I find one, I will let you know.

Terrifying? Yeah, but we've got to plan for it

I was in control and on point for the first five minutes in a meeting about Andrew last week. Then, what usually happens took place. The black wash overcame me. I felt submerged in a morass of deflating emotions. I defaulted to what I usually do. Focused on taking notes. Willed my analytics to take over.

This time, the meeting was with a financial advisor discussing Andrew's future – providing financially for his future after my wife and I depart this orb, talking about his future housing, discussing options regarding his care, caretakers, his health, who would oversee any funds we leave behind and – dare we dream – maybe some type of job, somewhere, somehow, some day.

I hate these ________ing types of meetings – and by 'these types of meetings' I mean I.E.P.s, therapy meetings, meetings with teachers, meetings with an endless line of specialists. I can't deal with it. I am weak there. For some reason, I can even handle him hitting me easier than being stuck in a room discussing what is wrong with my child. Nowhere to run. Nowhere to hide. The ugly truth.

But, I am fortunate because I have a wife who can handle those meetings. And, I have for the most part, bowed out of them, the last several years. Sure, call me weak. I can own it. But, spending three days in a severe depression following those meetings versus me not going and letting her relate to me the facts afterwards? Yeah, that is a fine trade-off. I can do that. Weak I am. ___ it.

But, back to the point of this entry. The meeting was about Andrew's future. He is nine now and whatever else happens, the future is coming at 60 seconds per minute for all of us. The adage by many special needs parents is may my child die one day before me. That is true. The thought of having our child as a grownup on his own and/or at the will of other people – despite how good their intentions or relations – is downright terrifying. If you don't live 15 minutes at a time, it will _____ you up pretty ____ good. And then ______ you up some more.

But, the bottom line is it is coming. We don't know what tomorrow may hold. How long will we live? Who will look after A when we are gone? How will his life be managed? Will there be any monies for A or will he be at the mercy of the whims of state and federal legislation regarding funding for special populations? Think about it? Yeah, terrifying.

As special needs parents, we've got to prepare. We've got

to explore options. Talk to one another. Talk to experts. See what works. What doesn't.

Yeah, it – forgive the vernacular – sucks to do it. It sucks the life out of you. It will scare you to death and depress you to think about it.

But, a few days worth of depression, in this case, is worth providing a lifetime of care for your special needs child.

So I encourage you to prepare. Anticipate. Plan. The only thing worse than planning for your child's future is not planning at all.

A plea for the special needs child sibling

Andrew's brother Peter has his despair by having a special needs brother. He has his anger, his resentment, his unanswered questions about his brother. He has these feelings when his brother hits him – and it happens at least twice a day minimum – when his brother attacks his parents, breaks dishes, yells, defecates all over the house, attacks Peter's friends when they come over and demands attention. And I understand. I empathize and I rarely chastise him. Because I have those thoughts and feelings, too. It is tough. No self-pity: Just a fact.

Peter's despair and anger haven't reached the levels of where mine have crested at times. Weeks wandering in the empty void, living in gray days, wondering what is the ________ing purpose of even trying. I hope he never does feel these emotions. God knows. And that is why, I work like the devil is on my heels to find him an outlet for his anger, his confusion, his frustration, his tears.

The past several years, I have worked tirelessly to find an outlet for him. He's played soccer twice, basketball once, tried tennis. Then there's been the acting, the music, the chorus. And we try them at least once to see if it takes. To see if the activity ignites something in him. Something to grab hold of. I won't push my 'typical' child into a sport he doesn't like, but I want him to try to experience it. So he can escape the confines of our house. So he can be connected to something 'normal' and, like I said, so he can find that outlet for his anger.

And, yet, he hasn't seemed to find it. And I need to accept that that is okay. Different kids find their passion at different ages. I was 11 when I became addicted to basketball. Until then, I was generally apathetic towards sports.

Perhaps he finds his outlets when he spends hours in his room having massive Lego wars and blasting the 'Star Wars' soundtrack loud as accompaniment. I don't know. Maybe that is his escape. His catharsis.

But, I want him to find it so desperately and I worry he won't. I don't want his anger to simmer. I have known that long-term anger. And it evolves into hate and it hollows you out.

So, I try to find that balance between pushing him and letting him find his way and wishing there was a ___________ ing guidebook on this path.

True Friends

You will learn who your true friends are. People will drop you like a bad habit when you have a special needs child. It is painful when they vanish, when their facade of an iron bond becomes nothing but a wraith-like illusion and their once-promising words of 'always' become empty. You will feel betrayed, sold out and hurt. You will learn deeper than you have ever before the raw meaning of the phrase "fair-weather-friend."

But you will find new support in other places. Places you would not expect. And people you would never expect, or seek out or think about in a million years. Maybe not new "friends," – bonds built on your past, shared experiences – but new allies, sympathizers, comrades and – dare I say? – selfless Christians. You will find them in church. In the grocery store. In the eyes of other special needs parents and one evening you find yourself having a conversation and a drink with another special needs dad of whom you have almost nothing in common with, except the strange alternative reality you both have inherited and live in. And, when that tends to define most of your paradigms, your time, your physical and mental boundaries, that is enough.

In the meantime, it can be overwhelming when someone reaches out with kindness. And beautifully, stupefying overwhelming. With that honest act of nothing to gain, just a desire to show you and your family love and comfort. When the neighbor you barely knows offers – though tentatively – to watch after your special needs child so you and your wife can go on a date. When a church member always makes a point to kiss him on the head. When the couple you see strolling the aisles of the hardware store, stop you, ask about your child and – even with your defenses high and your tongue ready to unleash a torrent of insults – you become diffused as they relate about a grandson they have with special needs. They leave you with a smile, a prayer and bit of understanding. You find this person who doesn't dress like you, talk like you, listen to your music or live in your world, loves you and loves your son unconditionally. And you realize and re-realize bonds made over drinks and jokes are fun. But, bonds made through shared pain and hope and understanding and love supersede all.

AMBUSHED

You never know when it will happen.

When you are in line at the grocery store when the woman asks you if you want to contribute to Special Olympics.

When you see the special needs adult holding onto their elderly mother's arm at Wendy's, staring vacantly at the menu, the cheery plastic prices a mocking juxtaposition to the scene.

When you are in Walmart buying clothes for the school year and your fears of your child finally transitioning to public school hits you in the gut. And you lean into the rack of Wrangler shirts, of all things to hide your face, your hand on the cool racks, your cheek buried in the imported fabrics smelling of new cotton.

The "it" is when you re-realize you have a special needs child. It is when you re-realize the gravity of not only what is happening, but the anxiety of what it is come. It is the re-realization that everything is not going to be all right in the end. It is the stiff wake-up call from whatever you've been hiding yourself in that day: Whether 'that' be staying busy, work, volunteering, arts or exercise.

So, you brace yourself. Stiff chin up. Man up, you tell yourself. _____ this, _____ those that don't understand my child, my world, my struggle. _____ it all.

And then, you shoddily piece your heart back together. You push back the venomous tirade lurking in your heart you want to unleash to the silent sky. You push your despair, your anger, your confusion deep, because even if you want to lose it, you can't.

You have to keep going.

And that is life to a degree. You can go about braced. Constantly ready for the storms of life to sneak upon you and gouge your mind's eye in an uppercut. You can remain inside your fortress, slink about in your cave. Or you can reach out, be brave and vulnerable and open to other's needs.

It is a hard balance, no doubt. There is no sure way to live in our strange existence as special needs parents, at least I haven't found one. If you have, chime in below. If not, hold fast, hang on and hang in. Hold fast.

Let me show you what I can do He told me

We got the looks, could sense the un-asked questions.

"Was your wife drinking when she was pregnant? Did she use drugs?"

"What did you do for God to punish you like this?"

"What terrible sin or crime did you commit?"

The answer to these questions is none of the above. My wife drinks less in a year than I do on a weekend. We did the prenatal vitamins, took the ultrasounds, were beyond safe with any toxins. Nothing showed up. Anywhere. We just hit the reverse lottery. At the time, he was only one in three children on the planet that had this certain chromosome deletion coupled with a hypo-plastic corpus callosum.

Why did this happen to Andrew? To us? To his brother? To our life? I don't know, but beyond all, I have to cling to John 9:1–3. On the bleakest and on the brightest days, it gets me through.

1 As [Jesus] passed by, He saw a man blind from birth. 2 And His disciples asked Him, "Rabbi, who sinned, this man or his parents, that he would be born blind?" 3 Jesus answered, "It was neither that this man sinned, nor his parents; but it was so that the works of God might be displayed in him."

I pray to hold onto that and to remember that this life and my purpose – real or perceived – is greater than myself.

It's Cri du chat awareness week

...and I could care less

Ouch, I can hear some of you say. That is a harsh title for an entry. Well, let me bring you up to speed. Cri du chat is the diagnosis/ailment/disability my youngest son Andrew suffers from. In a nutshell, as part of his diagnosis, he is missing part of his fifth chromosome which causes severe mental and physical development issues (just google it if you want more details.) So, why would I not care about this being a week to spread the word about awareness to his condition? Why would I sound apathetic about it? For one, I hate it. I hate that it exists and that my child and others suffer from it. I hate that I feel like it has completely screwed up my life and my family's life.

Also, I don't want to publicize my child's shortcomings, my own griefs and - real or perceived - what are I feel are my failures in this life.

Secondly, and, I think more importantly, I don't care about making this week a priority because one thing I have learned the past ten years being around other special needs families and special needs children is disability is disability. I say this with no disrespect towards any child or parent or sibling, but disability is disability. All of our children fight similar battles, are maligned with similar issues, fight the same battles for therapy, cope with similar sensory issues such as toilet training, behavior...yes, the list goes on and on...

And, us parents, too. We all tend to be in the same galaxy including everything from fighting for therapy for our children to trying to keep them a decent education. I have learned no disability is greater than another, and I find it rare for any parent to think it so.

I can't tell you the exact diagnosis of all of Andrew's friends, but I can probably tell you their favorite superhero or what makes them laugh or frustrates them. I can tell when I see them if they want me to hug them or want a high five.

Disability is disability.

Just like kindness is kindness.

Empathy is empathy.

Love is love.

Courage is courage.

Acceptance is acceptance.

10 things I've learned the last 10 years

Tomorrow marks Andrew's tenth birthday. Bittersweet...

Here are ten things I've learned in the last ten years.

1. The Church is full of hypocrites as the World is, but anyone who is willing to volunteer a couple of hours on a Sunday morning to spend with my disabled child is a saint. These people who truly believe in a morality and purpose greater than materialism and self-service donate their time so my wife, other son and I can try to find some hope in a service and fellowship. I have been severely blessed to meet many of these saints.

2. Andrew has taught and re-taught me the simple joys and pleasures of life.

3. Depression, rage and deflation will never leave. Will never be resolved. Or end. But they can be managed. You have to be conscious of them. Keep them at bay. At the

door. The best way to best them is to address them head on. Stay vigilant.

4. A special needs teacher is truly the hardest job on the planet. Period.

5. The teachers, volunteers and therapists who have helped my son along the way are some of the greatest people I know and, despite how may times I tell them, they have no idea that I hold them in such high esteem.

6. My sense of social justice has been reignited and, while I do try to keep my self-righteousness in check, I continue to be amazed and sickened by the politicians who align themselves with religion publicly, yet who channel tax money and resources into areas that don't need them while the least of these are left in the cold. I have not been ignorant of these issues, but the more I discover, the more disturbing it is.

7. As my friend Marie said, I do believe that special needs children have a direct connection to God. Their mind is unfiltered and uncluttered like ours and we can learn much from that perspective.

8. I have seen few things as beautiful as the smile on a special needs child's face or a look of joy in their eyes. They are all my heroes.

9. I've been to hell and back so many times I have frequent flyer miles.

10. I have yet to find God in the fire of a bush or have him visit me by the river in the night like Jacob, but I have seen him in the flight of the black butterfly, heard his words in the echoes of the thunder and seen him most of all through

the actions of other people toward Andrew and my family, and for that I am grateful.

PART
TWO

That's what she said

Let us linger with the lie

As my husband started pouring his thoughts and feelings into this, he asked me to go through some of our pictures to find some for him to post with his words. As I click through the hundreds of pictures stored on my computer, I am struck by a singular thought: Wow.

Pictures lie.

If a stranger looked through these mounds of memories, they would think our son, Andrew, was walking at a very early age. It's impossible to tell that he is leaning against his grandmother or the wall or the couch. They wouldn't know how bitter our older son, Peter, feels against this younger brother who is constantly biting and kicking and hitting him.

In the pictures of them sitting next to each other, they actually look like they love one another. There is even one of Peter reading to Andrew. How blessed we are to have cameras handy to capture the rare and wonderful and a delete option to erase the ugly.

Over the years I've gotten pretty good at identifying kids who have a diagnosis. I can even tell in pictures. Not because of the look on the child's face, but because of the placement of the parent's hands - over the chest or around the arm. An attempt to look natural while trying to keep said child from running away.

I know there are some who would say we should make more of an attempt to capture the ugly side of our lives in pictures, but, you know what, I am confronted with the ugly side every day. I will likely be confronted with it for the rest of my days. Give me the rare and wonderful.

Let me lock those moments into my head and heart to hold onto during the difficult times.

Let me fool the world with photos so that when they look at my children, they think of them as adorable instead of angry and cute instead of crippled. There are few humans on Earth who have to deal with brutal honesty more than we parents of broken children. Let us linger with the lie.

How to keep your marriage strong beneath the strain of special needs

Keeping a marriage healthy and strong can be tough for any couple. With the demands of work and out-of-control schedules making time for each other can seem, at times, impossible. So how does a couple manage to stay together and happy with the added stress of caring for a child with special needs? Here are ten steps that might help:

1) Communicate: From the beginning of our relationship, Special Needs Dad was insistent on the need for open and honest communication. This was difficult for me. I don't like to hash out issues. I prefer to think about ways I can fix them myself. However, I worked really hard to become a

better communicator, and that work paid off when Andrew was born. Andrew's Dad and I made the decision to be completely honest with each other without any judgment. That led to some pretty dark conversations that we would never share with another soul. But, it also cemented the fact that we have each other's back.

2) Pray for one another: There is a quote by C.S, Lewis that reads, "I pray because I can't help myself. I pray because I'm helpless. I pray because the need flows out of me all the time- waking and sleeping. It doesn't change God- it changes me." I can't imagine anything more beautiful than a man taking the time to pray over his wife and family. It's a humbling act that says, "God, I can't do this all by myself." When a wife prays over her husband, it tells him that his happiness, his future, his circumstances matter enough for her to beseech the Almighty on his behalf. As parents of special needs children there are so many things that are completely out of our control and beyond our understanding. But, as the Bible says, "Cast all your anxiety on him because he cares for you." (1 Peter 5:7)

3) Make time for each other: Making time for each other isn't easy. Not only is it expensive to go out to eat or see a movie, but babysitters are expensive and difficult to find. Going away on an overnight trip together is practically impossible. Thus far we've managed to get away for a few nights once a year, but it looks like we are going to have to find respite if we plan to do it this year, since Andrew is getting harder to handle. It's important, though, to be

reminded why you like this guy who plops down on the couch beside you at night. It's nice to remember there is something behind those kisses good-bye in the morning. When you think of all the effort, physically and fiscally, that people put into having extramarital affairs, don't you think it makes sense to use even half that effort to hold onto the relationship you have? Besides, who wants to break in a new spouse? Ain't nobody got time for that.

4) Overlook flaws and weaknesses: Over the past two weeks, our entire household has been sick. Luckily, I got sick first so I could take care of the others when their turn came around. When everyone finally got better and made their way back to school and work, I have to admit I did not use my free day to get the house back in order. Instead, I went to Walmart. And Big Lots. And The Dollar Tree. And Party City. Are you catching my drift? I let the laundry lay, the dishes soak and I spent the entire day running useless errands that could have waited and spending money that should have stayed in our bank account. After all that, my sweet husband sent me a fruit basket with a card that read, "Thank you for taking care of us." How does this man still love me? Does he not realize there are women out there who have houses that are actually clean? But, guess what? He's not perfect either. Sometimes he says things that make me want to pop him upside the head. He gets grumpy and unreasonable. He snores. But I still think he's the sexiest beast on the planet. Why? Because I've decided to overlook his flaws and weaknesses and appreciate his heart. I focus

more on his good points than I do on anything negative. And, I acknowledge that for every flaw he might have, I have at least ten more. Not to mention that I remain perpetually grateful for his love. I think that helps, too.

5) Have compassion: As a woman I tend to bear the brunt of most of this special needs stuff. Most of us do. We make the decisions about therapies and medicines. We travel to the doctor's appointments and we sit through the IEP meetings. It's easy for us to feel like we are carrying the heaviest of the burdens. I'm sure Andrew's dad feels similar. He is the one who had to pack away his dreams of moving up the career ladder, working in another state or country or accepting fellowships for exciting adventures overseas. He carries the weight of wishing he could fix this fractured life. He might even feel like he wishes he could walk away from it - so many do. It's not easy for any parent of a child whose future is uncertain. It's hard for a father to see a son who will likely never be able to provide for himself. It's hard for a mother to see a daughter who will never be asked to the prom or walk down a wedding aisle. No matter how the scales seem to balance, we must always keep in mind the hurt our spouse is enduring. When we and I got married we had the poem, "He Wishes for The Cloths of Heaven" by W.B. Yeats read at our wedding. It seems even more appropriate now.

It reads,

Had I the heaven's embroidered cloths,

Enwrought with golden and silver light,
The blue and the dim and the dark cloths
Of night and light and the half-light;
I would spread the cloths under your feet:
But I, being poor, have only my dreams;
I have spread my dreams under your feet;
Tread softly because you tread on my dreams.

Tread softly, friends.

6) Facilitate a relationship between your spouse and children: A happy family makes for a happier marriage. Your children, special needs or typical, need the individual attention of Mom and Dad whether it's having a date night, a movie night or a walk around the block. Mothers have a tendency to so encompass the life of their special needs child that sometimes it's difficult for dads to forge a meaningful relationship. Mom, take a step back and encourage Dad to spend some time with your special needs child. Whether it's signing them up for an special needs sports team or having a standing date to take the car to get washed. And, moms remember that your typical children need special time with you. It's so easy for them to feel excluded when all the attention is on their sibling. I recently went on a date night with my typical son. It was nice to go out to a restaurant where I could focus on the relationship between me and my typical son without the usual distractions. And not having to cook or worry about a babysitter? Bonus!

7) Do little things: Being a caretaker is exhausting especially when you're as disorganized as I am. However, I still try to remember to do little things for my husband. Sometimes I scrape the windows on his car on a cold morning. I pick up a fancy beer for him to enjoy. I let him sleep in on weekends. They aren't big things, but I think they remind him that I care. And, for his part, he takes my car to get gas or to get the oil changed. He brings me flowers. Sometimes he even brings me chocolate, which especially warms my heart because I think, "Maybe he really doesn't mind all this weight I've gained? " Never get so mired in the bog of duty that you forget to do nice things for your cutie. You can quote me on that.

8) Send them away: Sometimes I look at my husband and say, "Go. On. A. Man. Night." It's not because I don't miss him when he's gone, I just know that he needs some time away to gather his thoughts and repair his soul. On the same note, he tells me to call my friends and have a girls' night out. Most of my friends (okay, all of my friends) are mothers of special needs children, so we always relish having time to commiserate. Oh, the stories we tell. I'll be honest. When I'm not home the kids' bedtime routine is thrown into chaos, but, what the heck. It's one night! And, when either of us are gone, absence really does make the heart grow fonder.

9) Refuse to sacrifice your family on the altar of special needs: Life goes on. Your wife's uncle is never going to un-

derstand what your life is like so don't get mad at him when he says something ignorant. Your special needs child might never get to go skiing, but that doesn't mean your typical child shouldn't. You might want to empty the bank account to get your child an expensive therapy, but you still have to think about bills and retirement. Life isn't fair, but that doesn't mean we should bankrupt ourselves or alienate the people who care about us or limit the actions of our typical children in an attempt to make things fair. I'm not saying you should give up or stop fighting for your child. I'm just saying there are a lot of battles to fight, so choose wisely. This is especially pertinent to husbands and wives. We each think we know best what our children need, but do your best to stay on the same page and drop your sword when necessary.

10) Take care of yourself: If I had my way, I would eat donuts for breakfast, lunch and dinner and I might even take up cigarette smoking. I would thumb my nose at God. I would yell whenever someone made me angry, and I would kick holes in the walls when I'm frustrated. There is something about being faced with an overwhelming obstacle that, I think, makes us want to give up on everything.

You can't.

You don't have to be perfect. God knows I'm not. But, the best way you can be a great husband or wife is by being a great you. So, take care of yourself! Eat better. Get a hobby. (I'm still working on this one. My hobby seems to be hot tea, chocolate chip cookies and English dramas.) Find an outlet - writing, exercising, cooking. Listen to NPR or a book on tape. Call an old friend. Write a letter or make out a card and actually mail it. Do something that has nothing to do with special needs and remind yourself that you're interested and interesting and worthy to be loved.

In case you forgot already, you are worthy to be loved.

What it means to be Andrew's mom

This week is Cri du chat Awareness Week, so I figured I should do my part for the cause. However, as with any syndrome, every child with Cri du Chat is different. We are pretty much all told our children will likely never walk or talk and some, unfortunately, don't. We are very blessed with how far Andrew has come and how much he continues to progress. So, instead of giving an insight into the unpredictable symptoms of Cri du chat (otherwise known as 5p-), I thought I would say a little something about being a mom to my son who has Cri du chat:

Being Andrew's mom means listening to him play an out-of-tune ukulele…A LOT and watching A LOT of really bad ukulele players on Youtube. However, we also get to listen to him sing praise songs to God… that sometimes end up talking about his teddy bear.

Being Andrew's mom means we can't leave the house

without a pile of golden books and an armload of stuffed animals. It also means I get to revel in the knowledge that my child has a great imagination and can read!

Being Andrew's mom means having to change diapers on a nearly 9-year-old. It also means cleaning up poop from the walls, the sheets, the floor, etc. because, most usually, THAT doesn't seem to show up in the diaper. But, let's be honest, the floor wouldn't get mopped half as much otherwise.

Being Andrew's mom means worrying he isn't getting enough nutrition from his countless peanut butter and jelly sandwiches. It also means that my heart dances when I see him use his fork or spoon when he actually eats dinner!

Being Andrew's mom means he will eat any papers lying around. That's one way of cleaning them up!

Being Andrew's mom means I get scratched, bitten and I get my hair pulled…a lot. I also get snuggled, kissed and adored…a lot!

Being Andrew's mom means we can't go to many events we would like to participate in. It also means I always have an excuse to stay away from something I don't want to attend.

Being Andrew's mom means being woken up most nights at midnight and 4 a.m. However, it also means having a little cutie pie ramble into our room, turn on the lights and say, "Boy, am I glad you're here!" And, that's adorable no matter what time it is.

Being Andrew's mom means we have lots of gates and lots of locks. However, if a burglar ever does get in, he won't be able to escape before the police arrive.

Being Andrew's mom means sometimes feeling like I am going to lose my temper and understanding why so many parents do. It means wishing he could do things I know he wants to do. It means wishing I had the energy to keep up with his chaos.

But, it also means learning what unconditional love really is.

Adjust your feed -
INCREASE YOUR PEACE

Last night my nine-year-old special needs child climbed onto my lap and fell asleep. This happens most nights and, though he is probably a little too big for it, I enjoy these moments where I can snuggle with him without worrying he might bite me or scratch me or pull my hair. We're just together and I am aware of his great love for me, and I feel myself pour into him my great love for him. All was well. The troubles of the day were melting away. My thoughts and worries pushed aside as I lived vicariously through the characters on TV. Precious bedtime, the moment I sometimes wait anxiously for all day, had finally arrived. Then, it happened. I glanced at my phone one more time before heading to bed and I saw it. One of those Facebook posts. One of those - isn't my life grand, aren't my children beautiful and healthy, aren't I fabulous and skinny despite having given birth to all these wonderful kids - Facebook posts glared at me from my cracked phone. Suddenly, the sweet boy on my lap felt heavy, and I was reminded I was going to have to carry him to bed, medicate him, change his diaper and sit on him to brush his teeth.

On the way to his bedroom, I was going to have to pass by unfolded laundry, unwashed dishes, and I was going to have to walk over a dirty floor. In spite of the fact that I only have two children my world is chaos. It must be because I am so, so inadequate.

Don't get me wrong. I'm not usually a hater. It's just that I know some of these Facebook friends. I know their sins. I know the terrible things they've said and done. I know the hurtful things some of them have done to me! So occasionally I'm struck by the injustice of it all. That girl who did drugs all through high school and college now pictured with her gifted children. That person I know to be a racist enjoying a fabulous cruise when I'm lucky to get to the grocery store alone. That person who dropped me as a 'real friend' when my disabled son was born looking so darn perfect! And I wonder, do they think I deserve to change diapers on a nine-year-old? After all, they know my sins, too.

It happens so quickly, doesn't it? Our blessings start to look like burdens. Our silver linings get tarnished. We dig ourselves a hole, take up our position and prepare for a well-deserved pity party.

I felt that aching lump in my throat and thought, "Well, I'm never going to get to sleep now." Then, I thought about how much I love sleep. How much I deserve sleep. How my kid could interrupt my attempt at sleep at any time during the night. And, why am I going to miss out on my precious sleep? Because I'm comparing myself to people I never see or communicate with beyond social media?

I decided to take a few steps to ensure this doesn't happen again:

1) I acknowledged that social media is a tool to keep me connected to people I really care about.
2) I reclaimed my blessings. I imagined myself as a soldier taking a hill and planting my flag.
3) I gave thanks for what I have - my home, my family, my paid-off car.
4) I did the dishes.
And,
5) I hid some people from my feed.

I know what you're thinking. I should have gotten over myself and stopped being jealous! But something that all caretakers and parents of special needs children have to continually accept is that the moment we open our eyes in the morning, we face a big job ahead. We can't mire ourselves in the grime of our imperfections, but we can't ignore them either. Instead, we need to count our blessings, grab joy with both hands and, most of all, survive!

Most of us aren't perfectly equipped for this task. In fact, some of us are pretty poorly equipped. So we've got to stop beating ourselves up for what we don't have and can't do and start patting ourselves on the back for what we daily achieve in spite of the obstacles thrown in our path. Claim your blessings. Claim your peace and enjoy your life.

A Thanksgiving prayer

Dear God,

Today I pray for those of us who will travel long on little sleep. Who must explain to relatives why their child won't eat. We pray for those who want to visit and laugh, but instead have to walk the halls or the yard or even take a ride in the car.

I pray that if something is meant to be broken, it will be something unsentimental and cheap. That if someone's hair is to be pulled, it will be the least dramatic of the group and certainly, please God, not great-grandma when she only wants to give a hug. Most importantly, may any poop stay contained in the diaper and occur AFTER the meal.

Please let there be something our kids like to play with whether it be 'Paw Patrol' or Grandpa's foot massager.

Please let our child do at least one cute thing that will make Grandma feel like her prayers mean something.

Please help us to be quick to forgive silly arguments, snide comments and well-meaning cliches.

And God, though this day may sometimes be hard, let us view THIS Thanksgiving through the lens of the surreal and of good humor - that any idiosyncrasies will be inside jokes and any horror stories will simply be a great story to tell our special needs friends.

May this Thanksgiving be full of thankfulness and peace and love - unconditional love- which is the specialty of people like us.

Amen.

Our House in the Middle of our Street

Our house is different. It's not super different. It looks like any ordinary house from the outside, but there are elements about it that are...quirky. Quirky enough that when people come to visit they are off-put or frustrated by our small, but significant discords. For example, our pictures are hung really high. Our television hangs almost uncomfortably high up on the wall, too. Our kitchen is gated off and all the cabinets are childproofed. All the doors have safety locks except the knob on my special needs son's door, which has been turned around so it locks from the hallway. The toilet has a pair of barbecue tongs hanging next to it. Our silverware doesn't match. Our plates and bowls don't match, either. Neither our special needs son nor his typical brother's beds have frames and presently there are two balloons tangled around the ceiling fan that hangs from our vaulted ceiling. I have a perfectly good explanation for all of it. And when visitors get frustrated when they have trouble getting into the kitchen or leaving out the front door, I could sit them down and explain why things are the way they are. But I don't feel compelled to explain each quirk and I don't care very much if people understand. They don't have to live here!

In the same vein, when my son lays down on the floor in the grocery store, I don't get embarrassed. I didn't tell him to lay down. I didn't raise him to collapse every time we go out into public. I don't have to explain the fact that he is nine-years-old and wears a Superman cape… and diapers. I don't have to explain why I didn't freak out when I noticed he was eating the grocery receipt. I'm not rude. In fact, I make an extra effort to be a kind and friendly ambassador for the special needs community. But I find that friendliness is difficult when I am fraught with worry about what people are thinking about me and my son.

So I do my best not to worry about it, and most of the time I'm pretty successful. I think it takes practice.

Fortunately, in my experience, people are generally pretty nice. When they aren't kind, however, it can ruin your whole day. At those times, I have to remind myself that before I had my special needs son, I wasn't always the most sensitive person when it came to special needs people. I'll be honest: special needs people scared me a little. Regular people scared me a little. There is no way I could understand what this life as a special needs parent is like without experiencing it first hand, and neither can the confused and nervous and yes, rude, people you come in contact with every day. The only choice we have, the only way to find sanity on our strange and stormy sojourn, is to have mercy on their ignorance, find humor in the absurdity of our experiences and be what we are - different. If you can accept and embrace the things that make our journeys unique you'll be amazed at how much better you'll feel. Freer. Friendlier. Forgiving.

And at least, my special needs friends, we can take comfort in being different together.

What would they say if they could?

When our son was born we were told he would likely never talk.

He does. A lot. And with a fairly impressive vocabulary. I'm not saying that to brag. It's just a fact. Another fact is that in my friend group of special needs parents, my child is the only one who is verbal.

It makes me feel terrible. I feel guilty. I don't want him to stop talking, now mind you. I just want so much for their children to start.

What would they say if they could? I tend to think they would say many of the same things my son says to me. The regular stuff about wanting to play with my phone. The lines he recalls from the TV show, "Big Comfy Couch." The fact that he wants to "Eat chips...no crackers...no, a banana... where is my peanut butter sandwich!?!"

My son occasionally says things that seem rather out of the blue. Of late, he's said a few things that have particularly touched my heart. He's said these things many times, either when he's sitting on my lap or riding in the car. At times when I have no choice but to listen. I don't know where he heard them first, though I would like to think God whispered them into his ear, and because of who he is, he listened. I also imagine these are the things that nonverbal children would say, if they could.

1) "God made me." As the parent of a special needs child it's easy to get caught up in these words like a fish in a net. "If He made you, then why didn't He make you typical? Why would He craft something so imperfect?" When my son says this I often reply, "Yes, He did and I am so glad He made you, so I can love you." If you know anything about the love of a special needs parent for their child, you know it is the most powerful kind of love because it is unconditional. We love our children like God loves us- often not "because of" but "in spite of." Because we are all imperfect. Every one of us has special needs. But in spite of our deficiencies, we also have value and a purpose. So do our children. God made them to have value and a purpose.

2) "I am a gift from God." Sometimes my child doesn't seem like much of a gift from God, especially when I'm trying to shower poop off of him while he is pulling my hair and scratching me. However, I remember talking to one of my friends who was struggling with infertility and also worrying that, because of the many medications she had to take for her health, any child she might have would have special needs. (She later had a healthy baby boy.) I said, "I

would rather be a mother to my special needs son than not be a mother at all." I know not everyone feels that way and I completely understand why, but this job we have is a gift. I'm not one of those people who believes God chose me to be a special needs parent. On the contrary, I believe it was meant for me to be my son's mother and my son happened to be born with special needs. We live in an imperfect world and bad things happen. Sometimes chromosomes don't fall into place like they should. Brains don't develop properly. Spines are exposed. Proteins are misappropriated. Chemicals are out of balance. It's easy to look at people whose children seem perfect and wonder, "Why they deserve a better gift than we?" But our children don't care about those details. They can't apologize for who and what they are and why should they? They know, like all of us do, that they are meant to be loved and love is a gift.

3) "You are the best mommy ever!" Ha! What does he know, right? The best mommy ever would be way more patient. She would keep a cleaner house so you wouldn't have so many options of non-food items to eat and swallow. She would brush your teeth way more than once a day. She would diligently work on your therapy exercises. She wouldn't feed you pizza even though she knows your body doesn't like dairy. She wouldn't complain so much when you wake up at 4 a.m. How can this kid possibly think I am the best mother ever?

Because I'm his.

Sometimes it feels suffocating to be his, but no matter how often I falter, he is still going to think I am the best. It's humbling. No one else on this planet thinks I'm nearly that great. Some people don't even like me, if you can believe that. But to this kid I am the best. And to your kid you are the best. I can say without hesitation that your child would say that to you, if he could. If he wasn't hampered by his body's glitches and infirmities, he would look into your face and say:

"I am made by God to be a gift to you, and I am so lucky because you are the best!"

The world is full of hope ...sometimes you just have to trust

There was no way it was going to work. It was expensive, it was far away, and my son hadn't been away from me for that long since he was a baby in the NICU. I had the paperwork, but I didn't want to fill it out. What was the point? My child was not ready for camp.

Fortunately, the camp director didn't listen to me. She took my mostly, but not completely, filled-out paperwork and said, "Your son has a partial scholarship. Drop him off at camp at 2 p.m. on July 12th."

But...I...ok, fine. Be that way. You'll see.

The morning of camp, my sweet, not-so-little, ten-year-old boy climbed up into my lap and said, "Can I just stay home?”

This is never going to work, I thought. They are going to rue the day.

We arrived at Camp Hawkins, nestled in the foothills of the North Georgia mountains. I drove a bit too fast up a narrow dirt road to the campground, which consisted of two white cabins, a large aluminum activity center and a small swimming pool. My son fussed a little as we stood in the check-in line. Ok, actually he was yelling, “I want to go home!” A cheery-looking fellow with a beard appeared and said, “Hi, buddy. I’m your counselor, C.J. Let’s go see our room!” He trotted off with this perfect stranger waving as he went.

No hug.

No tearful goodbye.

Leaving his beloved mother, otherwise known as "chopped liver," to fight separation anxiety all alone.

Every day I waited for the inevitable phone call. I didn’t want to leave the house in case they called the home phone instead of my cell phone. I got a lot done. I cleaned out the laundry room. I cleaned the kitchen. I started a renovation project in the bathroom. And when I was working in one room, there wasn’t someone trashing another room at the same time.

Hey, I thought, this isn’t half bad.

On the last day of camp, I arrived after the awards ceremony had already begun. I scanned the room, but my son was nowhere in site. I thought to myself, this is probably way too overwhelming for him. During the show, I saw one young lady continuously spit in her counselor's face. The counselor would just smile and wipe it off. I saw a few campers in wheelchairs who looked like they would be much too medically fragile to be away from Mom and Dad. They were still alive and healthy. I saw some kids with their hands over their ears because of the noise, but no tears. Then I saw my not-so-little son happily sitting on the lap of his cheery camp counselor. He hadn't even noticed me come in.

The kids were getting awards for keeping a clean cottage and for the special things they excelled at during their time at camp. One little girl got an award for jumping in the ball pit. A young man received one for being really good at drawing. Another young lady got one for being friendly and welcoming. When every award was called, each child's counselor would jump up and cheer like they had just received an Oscar or an Olympic gold medal. The campers would beam. Finally, it was my son's turn.

"This award goes to a young man who makes sure every book is put back in its place. You don't have to worry about late fees when this librarian is on duty. The Book Hunter Award!"

My son LOVES books, so I knew it was him before they even said his name, although the 'putting books away' part threw me off a little. Camp Hawkins has a talent show on the last night of camp, so for my son's talent they spread books across the stage that he had to pick up and put back in a basket.

The Book Hunter Award is proudly displayed on the refrigerator. When someone comes over, he shows it to them. When Grandparents call, he tells them about it.

Camp was over.

We survived! I mean, he survived. And he not only survived, but he did just as well as any of the other campers. Plus, he got to ride horses and visit a fun park and go swimming. They even went to the movies, which he never tolerates at home. We gave C.J. a big hug and a gift card, because I figured he REALLY deserved it. I bought two $1 water bottles for $20 because I KNOW they really deserved it. And as we drove away, my completely untraumatized child waved goodbye to his friends, to the cabins, to the pool and yelled out, "Goodbye, Camp Hawkins! I love you!"

I don't consider myself a control freak. I want my child to try new things and be independent, but when your toddler is trapped in the body of a ten-year-old, it can be really hard to let go. Also, I think it's hard to imagine that there are people in the world kind and patient enough to deal with the behaviors and the diaper changes and the mood swings that we deal with every day. I mean, do you look at Facebook? Do you watch the news? Do you follow politics? People are mean to each other.

Not all people are mean. The world is still full of goodness and love. Camp Hawkins and places like it are evidence. So, don't be so afraid to trust your child and the people who want to care for your child that you miss out on the value of separation. Embrace goodness. It makes the world a much nicer place to live.

You can read more about Andrew's Dad and his adventures at www.specialneedsdadchronicles.com.

Made in the USA
Lexington, KY
13 June 2019